ENDURING WINTER

AT VALLEY FORGE

A HISTORY SEEKING ADVENTURE

by Eric Braun

CAPSTONE PRESS
a capstone imprint

Published by You Choose, an imprint of Capstone
1710 Roe Crest Drive, North Mankato, Minnesota 56003
capstonepub.com

Library of Congress Cataloging-in-Publication Data is available on the Library of
Congress website.

ISBN: 9781669058236 (hardcover)
ISBN: 9781669058205 (paperback)
ISBN: 9781669058212 (ebook PDF)

Summary: YOU are struggling to survive with the rest of the Continental Army
during the brutal winter of 1777–1778. The stark conditions in the camp at Valley
Forge have many soldiers doubting their cause and the leadership of General
George Washington. Step back in time to face the challenges and decisions that
real people faced during this pivotal time in history.

Editorial Credits
Editor: Mandy Robbins; Designer: Heidi Thompson; Media Researcher: Jo Miller;
Production Specialist: Tori Abraham

Image Credits
Alamy: Niday Picture Library, 37; DVIC: NARA, Cover; Getty Images; DEA
PICTURE LIBRARY, 31, Kean Collection, 71, mikroman6, 77, MPI, 44, pictore,
64, Stock Montage, 86, THEPALMER, 4, Universal History Archive, 12; Library
of Congress, 18, 24, 33, 57, 84, 94; Shutterstock: Amy Lutz, 58, Everett Collection,
80, Gabrieuska, 20, K Steve Cope, 40, Ken Schulze, 60, Marzolino, 49

Printed and bound in China. 5592

TABLE OF CONTENTS

About Your Adventure.........................5

CHAPTER 1
The Capital Is Lost 7

CHAPTER 2
Sold into War........................... 11

CHAPTER 3
Following the Camp 43

CHAPTER 4
The Horseman...........................73

CHAPTER 5
A Turning Point in the Revolution 101

Timeline of the American Revolution 106
Other Paths to Explore............. 108
Bibliography 109
Glossary 110
Read More 111
Internet Sites....................111
About the Author..................112

ABOUT YOUR ADVENTURE

YOU are on the front lines of history during the American Revolutionary War (1775–1783). Your decisions don't just mean the difference between life and death. They could change history forever.

Are you ready to dive into the past? What role would you play during this pivotal time in history? How might your actions make a difference? YOU CHOOSE which path to take. Will you survive and make your nation proud?

Turn the page to begin your adventure.

CHAPTER 1

THE CAPITAL IS LOST

YOU are losing hope. It has been about a year and a half since the signing of the Declaration of Independence in 1776. But at this moment, the thought of independence seems like a long-lost dream. The British army has defeated the Continental Army in a string of battles. And now, King George III's troops have taken over the city of Philadelphia, America's capital. As the weather turns colder, General George Washington's Continental Army flees the city to regroup over the winter.

Turn the page.

The army that straggles through the countryside now is far from professional. It's a haggard group of citizen soldiers with little experience. The patriots are losing battles to the highly trained British soldiers. Many are sick or injured. Few have enough clothes, shoes, or blankets for the coming winter. Hundreds of the soldiers' loved ones trail along as well. Most feel safer with the army because of all the British soldiers in the area.

The plan is to spend the winter at Valley Forge, about 23 miles northwest of Philadelphia. It had been an active community with ironworks and mills, but the British destroyed most of it in an earlier battle. General Washington has chosen the site because it's on high ground that is easier to defend. The nearby Schuylkill River will be a way to move supplies into camp. But as the army stumbles in and sees the ruins of the site, many can't help wondering if this was the best choice.

It's not just Washington's choice of Valley Forge that is in question. After the string of humiliating defeats, many men in the Continental Congress want Washington to be replaced as the commander of the army. Some officers are eager to replace him too. The future of the Continental Army feels uncertain. General Washington is not giving up hope, though. He won't let his army give up, either.

As winter creeps toward its coldest days, you feel like you're at a turning point in the war for independence. Victory or doom—both feel very possible.

- To be a recently enslaved Black soldier, turn to page 11.
- To be a camp follower, a woman who followed her husband to battle, turn to page 43.
- To be a mail carrier turned soldier, turn to page 73.

CHAPTER 2

SOLD INTO WAR

As the war for independence has dragged on, it has become more difficult for the Continental Army to find enough men to fight. Each colony is required to recruit a certain number of men, but not every colony has been able to find enough volunteers.

Many Black people joined the fight at the beginning. But Black enslaved people, like you, never had the freedom to choose whether to join the fight. You never had freedom at all. But your life is about to change.

Turn the page.

Enslaved men working in the fields

The colony of Rhode Island has paid your enslaver for you to become a soldier in the Continental Army. It is early morning as you climb into the cart with several other formerly enslaved men and ride away. Armed Continental soldiers ride with you. All of you are quiet.

Though you are free of your enslaver, you are not exactly happy. You are leaving your wife and baby behind. Will you ever see them again?

Later that morning, you reach a town and line up with the other men to be processed into the army. You're nervous about going to war. They tell you that you will be a free man after the war is over. But what if you don't survive? Or what if these men are lying, and you end up in chains again? You've learned not to trust anything a white man says.

As you reach the front of the line, you can see what is happening up ahead. Someone is scratching every new soldier's arm with a metal instrument until they break the skin.

"What's this?" you wonder aloud.

Turn the page.

A white man in army uniform answers, "Variolation." You must look confused because he goes on. "Smallpox is running through the army and killing people. The doctor scratches a small amount of the virus into your skin. You'll get a mild case, but then you'll be protected."

You're not so sure. They're purposely giving people smallpox? You don't trust white folks. Why are they really doing that?

"I don't want it," you tell the soldier, but he just shrugs.

"It's not optional," he says.

- To try to get out of the treatment, go to the next page.
- To get the variolation, turn to page 17.

You'll do whatever you need to do to avoid that scratch. When the soldier turns his back, you pretend you have to vomit. You're excused from the line to rest. While you rest, you are handed your uniform. After you dress, you skip the line and join the other new soldiers in a dining hall. No one notices.

The next morning, you begin the march to Valley Forge, where you'll be stationed for the winter. When you arrive, you stand at attention with the other soldiers. Your commanding officer looks over the group. "My name is Lieutenant Johnson!" he barks. You've heard that voice before. As he walks along the line of men, your fear is confirmed. Lt. Johnson is the son of your former enslaver. You despise this man.

Turn the page.

That evening, you chat by the campfire with some other formerly enslaved soldiers. One of them, a short man named Crosby, keeps looking at you. He seems to be sizing you up.

Later that night, you're about to go into your tent to go to bed when he quietly calls your name. You turn. "We have a plan," he says.

You scan the area in case any officers might be listening. It seems clear. "Who's 'we?'" you ask.

"Me and some of the others," he says. "We're going to escape this army first chance we get."

"Why are you telling me this?" you ask. This is a dangerous conversation. A Black soldier caught deserting could be enslaved—or killed. But Crosby seems to think it's worth the risk.

"You could join us if you want," Crosby says.

- To join Crosby's group, turn to page 20.
- To tell him to count you out, turn to page 22.

You might as well take the variolation. It's not worth causing problems with these white men. Besides, maybe it may help you stay healthy.

The next day, you march to Valley Forge, an encampment where you are going to spend the winter. You pitch your tent in an area with other Black soldiers. You learn that your commanding officer is Lieutenant Johnson, the son of the man who enslaved you. You're infuriated. You just can't get away from that awful family!

The next few days are filled with cutting timber to build a cabin and hours of military training. Then one afternoon before dinner, you are approached by a white soldier at your tent.

"Colonel Wood wants to see you," he says, referring to one of the higher-ranking officers in camp.

Turn the page.

Soldiers in Valley Forge

You walk across camp to the colonel's cabin. The large building has stables and a shop attached to it. When you walk inside, you are hit with an unusual feeling—warmth. The cabin is heated with two large stoves. The secretary sends you back to Colonel Wood's office.

From behind a large desk, he explains why you're here. "Lt. Johnson says you're strong, skilled with horses, and can build or fix anything."

You're surprised. The Johnsons never said a kind word to you in your life.

"Yes, sir," you reply.

"I need someone like that to work here," he says.

If you worked at the Colonel's residence, you would avoid combat. If the colonel likes you, he might even help you get your wife and son free. Plus, it's warm in here! On the other hand, you don't trust Johnson. Why has he been talking you up? What does he get out of this? And how will the other Black soldiers feel if you move over here? This won't make you any friends among them.

- To join Colonel Wood's residence staff, turn to page 23.
- To stick with the rest of the soldiers, turn to page 25.

You don't say a word to Crosby. You simply nod your head. He understands—you're in.

Over the next few days, you sneak food into your tent. One day after breakfast, you hide a biscuit in your tent. When you come back out, you are face-to-face with Lt. Johnson.

A recreation of soldier tents

"I've been watching you," he says. "You've been hiding food. Why?"

"I enjoy an evening snack, sir."

"Evening snack, is it?" he says. "So, if I look in your tent now, I won't find a stash of food?"

"A stash, sir?" It's clear he knows something is up, but you play dumb. "No, sir, no stash."

That night, by the fire, Crosby is all over you.

"What was that all about?" he asks.

"He's onto us," you say. "He knows we've been stashing food."

- To go through with the escape plan, turn to page 27.
- To call it off because it's too dangerous, turn to page 28.

"Your secret's safe with me," you tell Crosby. "But I'm not going."

"Suit yourself," Crosby says.

The next day, Lt. Johnson asks for volunteers to go foraging and hunting for food. You raise your hand.

The hunting mission is successful. You kill three deer, yourself. Johnson realizes that you are good at this and sends you out again. On a couple occasions, when you are out hunting, you consider escaping. But you never do. The only way you'll ever see your family again is if you stay here, survive this war, and find a way to buy their freedom. And in the meantime, it feels good to be recognized for your hard work and strong skills.

THE END

To follow another path, turn to page 9.
To learn more about Valley Forge, turn to page 101.

You can't pass up the opportunity to sleep in a warm cabin. And doing this may even help you reunite with your family.

"Thank you, sir," you say. "I'd be honored."

Over the next week, you care for horses, fix a gate, and begin building an extra room next to Colonel Wood's office. One day you overhear Wood talking to some other men in his office.

"He's incompetent!" Wood says. "He thinks he's a king, so we must knock him off his throne."

You realize they are talking about General Washington. Colonel Wood previously served General Horatio Gates before being transferred here. You know that there are some officers and members of the Continental Congress who are trying to get Washington replaced as the leader of the army. They say he has been a failure.

Turn the page.

General Horatio Gates

You don't agree with this. Though the army has suffered some defeats, the men respect and admire Washington. You've heard about many of his victories too. You think he is the right man for the job.

But could a change happen if these men are allowed to keep plotting? What can you do about it anyway?

- To try to get word to Washington about what you heard, turn to page 30.
- To mind your own business, turn to page 34.

In the end, it comes down to one thing. You hate Lt. Johnson. You don't want to work for anyone who is friends with him.

"I am honored, sir," you say. "But I feel my skills are better suited to the ranks."

"Very well," Colonel Wood says. "Dismissed."

You return to your unit, which is a mishmash of blacksmiths, farmers, city dwellers, seaside sailors, and more. Many of the men are immigrants with few resources. Some speak little or no English. There are many Black men like you, as well.

With a group this diverse, folks don't always get along well, especially when food is short. You have seen several arguments turn into physical fights.

Turn the page.

However, what bothers you most is the way you are treated by some of the southern white men. They think they are better than you. They resent a free Black man being in the same army as them. Most of these southerners watch you with suspicion. It all comes to a head one morning at breakfast, when a man named Turley spits in your food.

"What do you think about that?" he says. You stand, and he balls his fists at his side. Other men at the table—both Black and white—stand too.

- To fight Turley, turn to page 35.
- To let it go, turn to page 37.

"If we're going to do this, we better do it tonight," you say.

Crosby agrees. Johnson might wait a little while to get more evidence, but not too much longer.

That night, the four of you abandon your posts and run out of camp. You travel all night. Just as the sun is coming up, you see a man on horseback riding toward you.

You stop. Three other men come up behind you, also on horseback.

"Who are you?" the man in front of you says. He is a Native person, but he speaks English. He might be part of one of General Washington's scout units made up of Oneida and Tuscarora warriors. Washington sends them out to capture British soldiers—and deserters.

- To try to talk your way out of this, turn to page 39.
- To make a run for it, turn to page 40.

"He might have someone watching us right now," you whisper, looking around. "It's too risky."

You can tell Crosby is disappointed and angry. One of the other men pipes up. "He's right. We have to call it off."

You go into your tent and eat all the stashed food. The next few weeks, you train harder than ever. If you're going to be in this army, you are determined to be as strong and successful as possible. But one night, after a hard day of drills, you fall down in the snow. Crosby helps you up.

"I must be worn out from working so hard today," you say. You're afraid it's more than that, though. You don't feel quite right.

"You're hot," Crosby says, feeling your forehead.

He pulls you into your cabin, which you recently completed. You sweat all night and have wild, feverish dreams. You can't drill the next day. A medical officer says that you have smallpox. You won't be getting out of bed for days, maybe weeks. Maybe never. You think about that variolation you refused to take. Maybe that was not the best choice.

THE END

To follow another path, turn to page 9.
To learn more about Valley Forge, turn to page 101.

In your time at Valley Forge, you have made friends with a man who works in Washington's residence. His name is Burton. You tell him what you heard.

"The general is aware of the conspiracies," Burton says. "I will tell him about Colonel Wood. This may be new information to him."

For several months, you wonder if your information was helpful or not. What you do know is that things are getting better in camp. Washington has improved supply lines, so the camp has more food and other goods. The army has transformed into a strong, disciplined unit.

That spring, an alliance with France is announced, lifting everyone's spirits. Their assistance will be very helpful. Finally, in June, Washington's spies learn that the British plan to move out of Philadelphia. He sends troops to Monmouth, New Jersey, to confront them.

American artillery in the Battle of Monmouth

By this time, you are disgusted with Colonel Wood and request to be a part of the battle. You perform well, taking several British prisoners, but you are shot in the leg.

Turn the page.

Weeks later, while recovering in a hospital, a nurse stops by. "You have a visitor," she says. Several armed men enter the room. Then General Washington walks in. You are honored. He walks to your bedside and shakes your hand.

"Thank you for all you've given to the cause," he says, looking you in the eyes. Something tells you he is not only talking about your injury. Perhaps your information really did help him keep his position. You are proud of all you've done for this new nation.

Because of your injury, you can't fight anymore. But you are a respected veteran. When the war is over, you find a job and begin saving your money. It won't be long before you can buy the freedom of your wife and son.

THE END

To follow another path, turn to page 9.
To learn more about Valley Forge, turn to page 101.

General George Washington

It's too risky for a Black man to go behind the back of his white boss. If Wood found out, the punishment could be anything.

You keep your mouth shut. As the weeks go by, you tire of Colonel Wood. He is arrogant and bossy. He makes cruel jokes about sending you back into enslavement. It's hard to work for a man you don't respect, so you begin to purposely do bad work. Eventually, Colonel Wood fires you. You're sent back to live with the other men.

It is cold in your cabin. You go back to drilling, marching, and preparing for battle. Part of you misses the more comfortable life you had in Wood's residence, but you are glad to be away from him.

THE END

To follow another path, turn to page 9.
To learn more about Valley Forge, turn to page 101.

Turley smirks at you, as though he knows you won't stand up to him. You call his bluff and punch him in the stomach. While he's doubled over, you hit him in the mouth. He stumbles back before lunging at you.

You're getting the better of him when a couple of his friends join in. One pulls you off Turley. Suddenly, several Black soldiers join the fight. You break free and hit Turley again, knocking him out.

You look around. At least a dozen men are in this fight. By the time the officers break it up, several men have broken noses, broken fingers, and bloody lips. Turley has come to and is trembling on the floor. He eyes you with disgust and hatred.

Turn the page.

Your heart sinks. You know it was a mistake to fight. You let your pride get the better of you. When punishments are handed down, you are enslaved again. You don't think it's fair. You were only standing up for yourself. But the world has never been fair to you.

THE END

To follow another path, turn to page 9.
To learn more about Valley Forge, turn to page 101.

As a Black man, you know you are seen as a second-class soldier by all the white men, even those who are kind to you. If you get into a fight with a white man, you will lose even if you win.

You muster all your dignity, pick up your plate, and dump it in the trash. Turley continues taunting you, calling you racist names and trying to pick a fight. You avoid him the best you can. It's humiliating, but eventually he leaves you alone.

The ragtag Continental Army

Turn the page.

That spring, you and Turley are part of a unit sent to cut off the British in Monmouth, New Jersey, as they march from Philadelphia. You surprise them and send them into retreat.

You fight bravely and take back the city of Philadelphia. Turley is shot and killed in battle. You have mixed feelings about this. You don't wish harm to your fellow soldiers. So you're ashamed to admit that you feel relief knowing you won't have to deal with Turley anymore.

THE END

To follow another path, turn to page 9.
To learn more about Valley Forge, turn to page 101.

"Hello!" you say, as nicely as you can. "We are scouting for the general. Have you seen any redcoats in this area?"

The man in front of you gives a short laugh. "Why would the general send you to scout in the same place where he knows we are already scouting?"

"Oh," you say. "We're scouting for food."

The man in front of you signals to the men behind you. Suddenly, several guns are pointed at you.

"Tie them up," says the leader. You are captured. You don't know what your punishment will be for deserting. You can only pray for mercy.

THE END

To follow another path, turn to page 9.
To learn more about Valley Forge, turn to page 101.

You dash into the woods, hoping to shake them. Crosby and the others are right behind you. Branches slap your face, but you must keep running.

The sun is high in the sky by the time you finally stop to catch your breath. You sit quietly and listen. You don't hear the scouts, but that doesn't mean they're not nearby. You follow the creek north.

By nightfall, you reach a safe house that Crosby had arranged for, but when you tell them about the scouts, they refuse to let your group stay the night. If they are caught hiding deserters, the punishment would be as bad for them as it would be for you. They pack you some pork and bread and send you on your way.

For the next several days, you and your companions travel by night. Your only hope is to make it to Canada, which has remained loyal to Great Britain. No one there will turn you into the Continental Army. But you will always be wanted in America. You're afraid you'll never see your wife and son again.

THE END

To follow another path, turn to page 9.
To learn more about Valley Forge, turn to page 101.

CHAPTER 3

FOLLOWING THE CAMP

You and your husband, Lawrence, were married last spring. You own a farm in Delaware, and you have built a nice life. You're not rich, but you make do.

You both believe that America should be free of British rule. In the fall, Lawrence joined the Continental Army. You were proud of him. You stayed home to run the farm the best you could.

Turn the page.

An early American farm, around 1775

Then the British took Philadelphia. The
Continental Army tried to take back the city,
but they failed. You received a letter from
Lawrence saying that his unit was fleeing
Philadelphia to spend the winter at Valley Forge.
He sounded uncertain, maybe even afraid.

You decide to follow Lawrence because you are pregnant with your first child. You would feel safer by his side. You hire a neighbor to look after the animals on your farm. You pack your mule with food, blankets, and other supplies and leave.

You meet the marching army a few miles northwest of Philadelphia. Many other wives and children are also following the army. They help out in the camps and lift the spirits of the troops.

You quickly make friends with some of the other women. They warn you to stay out of General Washington's sight.

"He doesn't like womenfolk in camp," one woman says. Like you, she leads a mule packed with supplies. Ahead of you, a group of two women and several children ride in a squeaky cart.

Turn the page.

Apparently, the general is not happy with the families following the camp. He worries about feeding them. He worries they will be a distraction to the soldiers. He worries about protecting everyone in an attack. You realize these are all fair points. You and your new friend are determined to prove that you will be assets to the army, not burdens.

Finally, you arrive in Valley Forge. It is very disorganized. You help Lawrence pitch his tent and move some of your supplies inside. Then you report to a clerk who is assigning jobs.

You can work as a nurse or a laundress. As a nurse, you'll have an increased risk of catching a disease, but the pay is a little better.

• To be a nurse, go to the next page.
• To be a laundress, turn to page 49.

You like the idea of helping the men directly, and the extra pay is a bonus. Currently, the infirmary is in a large tent, but General Washington has made building a cabin a top priority. While the cabin is built, you see people in the tent with smallpox and other illnesses. You see men with frostbitten fingers and toes. One chopped off the tip of his finger while milling wood. Another has broken his ankle while doing military drills. Everyone is hungry and cold. As winter goes on, supplies run low.

You and Lawrence are hungry. Though you are earning extra money, there is no food to buy. Washington urges patience. Things will get better, and you believe him. But when?

You're treating a friend of Lawrence who has been ill. You've just told him to return to his tent when he grabs your wrist.

Turn the page.

"Thank you for your care," he says.

"You're welcome," you say.

He doesn't let go of your wrist. He looks around. No one is listening, so he continues, "Tonight, me and Farley are going to the farmhouse up yonder to find something to eat. You and Lawrence can join us, so you don't starve!"

The locals have already given all the food they can spare to the army. Washington has ordered soldiers not to take any more. Normally, you would never disobey a direct order. But you're constantly hungry, and a baby is growing inside you.

• To join them, turn to page 52.
• To refuse to join them, turn to page 54.

Being a nurse would expose you to too many diseases. You don't want to risk that while you're pregnant. You choose to do laundry, even though it is very hard, physical work. You stand over a boiling kettle stirring uniforms and blankets. You wring them out and hang them. After just two days, your hands are chapped raw.

A laundress

Turn the page.

Sometimes, officers' wives drop off or pick up laundry. There is a distinct class division among the women in camp. Lower-class women, such as yourself, are working for wages and living in tents while you build your own cabins. The officers' wives are referred to as "ladies." They live in cabins with their husbands and don't do any work. Not one of *them* has chapped hands.

One night, some of the officers and their wives put on a play for the other officers and ladies to watch. The soldiers and their wives are not invited, but you can hear them singing. It makes you angry.

A week later, a soldier is found dead in his tent from cold and starvation. He was a free Black man. This is the first person to die since you arrived at Valley Forge, and it causes a change in camp.

You're not the only one who noticed how well certain people have it compared to the rest. Many men and women are frustrated, and some are talking about deserting the army and going home.

You still believe in the cause, but you sure could use an extra blanket. You and Lawrence shiver every night. You wash dozens of blankets a day, and most of them are for those "ladies" and their husbands. Would they even notice if one went missing?

- To steal a blanket, turn to page 56.
- To decide not to risk it, turn to page 58.

That night, you tell Lawrence about the plan.

"I don't know," he says. "I could face serious punishment."

"Think of the baby," you say, rubbing your belly.

Lawrence nods. "You're right," he says.

Late that night, you and Lawrence find Farley and his friend Hassler near the edge of camp. The four of you creep up to a farmhouse down the road. You stand watch out front, while Lawrence and Hassler sneak into the chicken coop.

Farley goes up to the door of the house and pushes it open. You don't like that one bit. The house is too risky. Sure enough, the floor creaks under his steps. Suddenly, a lantern shines in an upstairs window. You whistle, which is the signal to get out.

Lawrence and Hassler come running out of the barn with some eggs in a sack. Farley dashes out the door of the house as a gunshot goes off. He yells and falls to the ground. You have to leave him. The rest of you run back to camp and divide up the eggs.

The next morning, there's a big commotion as the farmer comes into camp with the injured Farley in his cart. There is an investigation, and you and Lawrence are soon discovered. Both of you are whipped and kicked out of camp. You are still hungry, and now you have to walk all the way home.

THE END

To follow another path, turn to page 9.
To learn more about Valley Forge, turn to page 101.

You're very hungry, and you're worried about your baby's health. But the risk is not worth it. If you're caught and kicked out of camp, you could starve to death.

Thankfully, the army's foraging parties start having some success. They are coming back with deer, rabbit, and other meat. In addition, some local farmers willingly donate more food, mostly potatoes and other vegetables they've saved from harvest time.

One morning, a hunting party comes back with an injured peasant they came across while hunting ducks. The man was lying in the mud with a fever. He's brought under your care in the infirmary. As you nurse him back to health, he says some things that make you suspect he's not in favor of independence. One day, he's talking about General Washington, and he shakes his head in disgust.

"What do we want to do, trade one King George for another?"

Among his possessions are a pistol, a compass, and two maps of the area. You suspect he might be a British loyalist. Should you leave the man be so he can recover or report him to an officer?

- To leave him be, turn to page 60.
- To report your suspicion to an officer, turn to page 62.

You've had enough of the unfair treatment. You're working hard for the revolution, and you deserve to be warm. The next day, you hide one of the blankets in some bushes. That night, when it's dark, you come back for it. But when you bring it back to your tent, Lawrence gets angry.

"What are you thinking?" he whispers. "We'll be run out of here!"

"Let them run us out," you whisper back. "We deserve basic warmth, don't we?" The two of you argue, but in the end, you go to bed under the extra blanket. For the first time since you arrived in camp, you sleep comfortably. Lawrence is not quite so angry in the morning.

Soon, your own cabin is complete. You move into it along with 11 other people. It's warmer than the tent but crowded, and you're still very hungry. Diseases, such as smallpox and dysentery, are common.

Some soldiers have been deserting the army, going to Philadelphia, and surrendering to the redcoats. Their plan is to be thrown in jail, where they hope to be fed and clothed. You are getting desperate, and you're going to have your baby in a couple months. Do you really want to be in this cold camp with no food when you do?

Dire conditions in Valley Forge

- To turn yourself in to the British, turn to page 64.
- To keep sticking it out, turn to page 66.

You decide not to risk it. Besides, things are getting better, little by little. Washington has promised that supply lines will be operating more openly soon.

Unfortunately, Lawrence soon gets very sick with a fever and red spots on his neck, armpits, stomach, and back. You are certain it is smallpox. The rules on this are strict. People with smallpox must be moved to a special hospital. There, they will be isolated from the rest of camp.

Cabins at Valley Forge

The hospital is known to be filthy and filled with the moans of dying men. Most of the people sent there die. You can't let him go there, so you try to keep his illness a secret. Lawrence stays in bed, missing drills and assignments.

Soon, your cabin is complete. You are set to move into it with 11 other people. If Lawrence lives with these other men, he's putting them at risk. You and the baby are at risk too, but you love Lawrence enough, that it's worth it to you. You doubt the other men would feel the same way.

- To send Lawrence to the smallpox hospital, turn to page 68.

- To stay with Lawrence in a separate tent, turn to page 70.

Surgical tools used during the Revolutionary War

Your job is to nurse people back to health, not to be an informant. You continue taking care of the man, and he turns out to be friendly. He chats with several of the sick and injured soldiers, asking them about their jobs and more.

When he is healthy enough, he takes a walk around camp before returning to sleep in the hospital. The next day, he thanks you for caring for him and walks out of camp with a small bundle of food that the hospital gave him.

The next morning, someone starts shouting at the other end of the camp. You hear running soldiers and more yelling.

That night, when you return to your tent, Lawrence tells you what happened.

"Somebody stole some rifles last night" he says, "They knew exactly where to find them and how to get in and out unseen."

"Who could have done that?" you ask. You may never know for sure, but you have an idea of who it could have been.

THE END

To follow another path, turn to page 9.
To learn more about Valley Forge, turn to page 101.

That night, you walk over to Lt. Rushin's cabin and knock. One of the upper-class ladies answers.

"Can I help you?" she asks.

"I have something to report to the lieutenant," you say. "I think he'll find it useful."

The lady tells you to wait outside and shuts the door. A few minutes later, she returns and invites you in. You tell Lt. Rushin what you suspect.

"He keeps asking the other patients questions about tactics and what their assignments are," you say. "It's odd."

Lt. Rushin's eyebrows arch up at your news. "You did the right thing," he says. "I will take care of this."

The next morning, the sick peasant is not in his bed. You ask the night nurse about it, and she tells you that some officers took him for questioning. Later that day, Lt. Rushin and General Washington come into the hospital and find you.

"I want to personally thank you," Washington says. "That man was a British spy. We're lucky to have caught him."

Both men shake your hand. You are beaming with pride when they leave. Not only did you help the cause of the revolution, but you showed General Washington that women can be of real service.

THE END

To follow another path, turn to page 9.
To learn more about Valley Forge, turn to page 101.

You would do almost anything to fight for independence if you only had yourself to consider. But you can't go on putting your baby at risk. You decide to surrender yourself to the British in Philadelphia. Lawrence won't let you go alone. The two of you save some food and map your path.

Independence Hall in Philadelphia

It takes a couple days to reach Philadelphia. There, you turn yourselves in as members of the Continental Army. You are thrown into a cold, crowded, dirty jail cell.

Unfortunately, the rumors about there being food here don't appear to be true. You're fed even less than you were in camp, and the jail is not heated. To feed yourself, you eat the lice off your own head, and you eat what little grass you can pull from the prison yard. When the time comes for you to give birth, you are too weak. Both you and your baby perish.

THE END

To follow another path, turn to page 9.
To learn more about Valley Forge, turn to page 101.

You're too loyal to Washington to give up now. You know he is working hard to improve the conditions in camp. You trust that things will be better.

At first, things only get worse. Food supplies remain low. Some weeks later, the weather warms a little, and then you get rained on. The streets of the encampment are muddy, then frozen and rutted, then muddy again.

In February, the Continental Congress starts coming through with regular shipments of supplies. When everyone is eating better, the mood improves.

Lawrence is looking fit, strong, and ready for battle. And you are glowing with health. You'll be ready when it's time for the baby to come.

By June, Washington has learned that most of the redcoats are abandoning Philadelphia. He sends a large part of the army to confront them at Monmouth. He sends a smaller unit into Philadelphia to reclaim the city from the few remaining British troops. Lawrence is assigned to Philadelphia. You join him and his unit and help by arming cannons.

When the battle is over, Philadelphia is back in colonial control. You enjoy walking the streets of the city. You pass by a jailhouse where the redcoats had kept prisoners of war and shudder at the awful conditions. That's where you would have been if you had turned yourself in. You're glad that you came to Philadelphia as a winner in battle instead of a prisoner of war.

THE END

To follow another path, turn to page 9.
To learn more about Valley Forge, turn to page 101.

There is only one right thing to do. Lawrence must go to the smallpox hospital. It's proper protocol.

You exchange notes with him almost every day. At first, he is hopeful that he's getting better, but soon it is obvious that he's not. He is dead within two weeks.

By now, you are too pregnant to travel alone, so you stay in the cabin with the others. In the coming weeks, Congress starts sending more food, blankets, and other supplies. You continue going to work as long as you can. It's not long before your pregnancy makes it too hard for you to lift the wet, heavy garments.

You have your baby in May, a healthy little girl. You name her Laura. The people in the cabin all pitch in to help take care of you and the baby. They bring you food and help you in every way.

Soon, though, the camp grows quite lively. The army is packing up and getting ready to leave for battle. You load up your belongings on your mule and strap little Laura to your chest.

It's time to start the long walk home to the farm. You miss your husband dearly, but you're proud that he joined the fight for independence. You hope that your daughter will grow up in a nation free of British rule.

THE END

To follow another path, turn to page 9.
To learn more about Valley Forge, turn to page 101.

You don't want to send Lawrence away to die alone. You don't want to expose the men in the cabin to smallpox either. Any man who hasn't had the disease yet or who didn't get a medical treatment called variolation would be at risk. So the two of you stay in your tent. Lawrence lies coughing and talking wildly in his fevered state.

As the days pass, his condition worsens. Eventually, you change your mind. The hospital may be a scary place, but Lawrence isn't getting any better here. You must take him there.

By then, however, it's too late. Lawrence dies the day after his transfer. Worse yet, you are coughing and weak. Red sores appear on your neck and armpits. It's clear you have smallpox. You and your baby may not survive either.

THE END

To follow another path, turn to page 9.
To learn more about Valley Forge, turn to page 101.

People struggling to survive in Valley Forge

CHAPTER 4

THE HORSEMAN

You are one of the more skilled horsemen around. You made your living delivering mail all over the countryside by horseback. In your job, you met many people and saw much of the land. You came to really love this country, and you long for it to be independent.

That's why you joined the Continental Army under Brigadier General Casimir Pulaski, a Polish military hero and expert with light horse brigades. A brigadier general may be the lowest-ranking general, but you would follow Pulaski anywhere.

Turn the page.

Under Pulaski, you fought many battles and almost always came out on top. You love serving under him. By the time you ride into Valley Forge for the winter, you are known as an expert horseback fighter.

Confident because of your previous successes, you are hungry for more combat. Independence cannot be won soon enough.

Unfortunately, it appears it will be a long, cold winter in Valley Forge. No battles. No glory. Just waiting. Soon, supplies dwindle.

Washington is looking for ways to stretch resources. His solution is to send detachments to other locations, so he won't have to feed the soldiers. He's especially eager to send some of the horsemen away. It would spare him feeding the soldiers and their horses.

Washington sends an officer to speak with you and a few of the other men from Pulaski's brigade.

"Men," he says. "Because of your history of valor, General Washington is letting you choose. You can go with one of these detachments and live in the countryside for the winter. Or you can stay in camp but give up your horse, which would be sent elsewhere for the winter."

You're afraid that if you go away, you won't see battle for months. If you stay, you might have a better chance of seeing action. But you'd have to do it without your horse.

• To be part of a detachment, turn to page 76.
• To stay in camp without your horse, turn to page 80.

You agree to go. You'll probably be waiting no matter what. You might as well keep Poppy, your horse.

You set out on your journey to Trenton, New Jersey, the next morning. You stop for lunch along the side of the road, and Pulaski checks his maps and compass. He points to a small forest clearing on the map.

"This is a small community of British loyalists," he says. "Our spies have pinpointed them."

"What do you propose?" you ask.

Pulaski smiles. "Washington has given me permission to do anything while on detachment that will frustrate the loyalists. We're going to get us some more horses," he says.

Turn the page.

Revolutionary War soldier encampment

Stealing their horses would certainly frustrate them, you think. The men nod and laugh.

That night, you sneak into the small settlement. Pulaski and several other men keep watch while you and the others untie the horses in the corrals and lead them out. You calm the horses to keep them quiet, and nobody wakes up as you sneak out.

You reach Trenton with a large group of horses, only to realize there isn't enough grass around to feed them. Pulaski divides the crew into smaller units and sends each one to different parts of the countryside.

Your unit is assigned to guard a road into Philadelphia. The city is held by the British. Your job is to prevent loyalists from bringing supplies into the city for the redcoats. After several days, you realize that a couple of the soldiers in your unit have been allowing loyalists to pass through.

"What is this?" you ask.

"They're okay," a soldier named Donovan says. "I checked them out."

You realize that Donovan and his buddy are taking bribes. The loyalists pay them, and they let them through with supplies for the enemy.

You've always liked Donovan. You doubt he would let anyone dangerous pass through. And maybe you could get some of the money he's collecting. Still, he's disobeying orders.

• To report these men to Pulaski, turn to page 81.
• To join in the scam, turn to page 83.

You hate to give up the cavalry, but you don't want to hang out in some town or countryside and wait all winter. This is where General Washington is. He must be planning battles soon enough.

"I'll stay here," you tell the officer.

"Fine," he says, stroking his mustache. "I need infantry soldiers and scouts."

Soldiers around a campfire at Valley Forge

- To join the infantry, turn to page 85.
- To be a scout, turn to page 87.

"What you are doing is treason," you say to Donovan. "Have you no shame?"

Before Donovan or the other man can answer, you climb onto Poppy and ride away. The next morning, you reach Trenton and report to Pulaski. He is stationed at an inn. You tell him what happened.

"I knew it!" Pulaski says, slamming his fist on the table. You stay with Pulaski at the inn for the next few days, while he sends word to Washington about the men taking bribes.

You enjoy waiting here. The inn is warm, and the food is plentiful. You hear back that Washington has sent investigators. In the meantime, you will stay with Pulaski.

Turn the page.

Over the next few months, you and Pulaski move to different posts and carry out missions at each one. In March, Pulaski forms Pulaski's Legion, a cavalry brigade. You are a key member. You fight by his side in many battles over the years until Pulaski is killed in a battle in Georgia. When the war ends, you retire from the military a decorated hero.

THE END

To follow another path, turn to page 9.
To learn more about Valley Forge, turn to page 101.

"Either cut me in on this operation, or I report you," you say.

Donovan is happy to cut you in. Though you feel guilty disobeying orders, you like the extra money. You take some of the travelers' food as well. You're eating well and socking away cash.

One morning, as a light snow begins to fall, two horsemen approach you on the road wearing the colors of the Continental Army. They are officers. When they reach you, one of them dismounts.

"Which one of you is in charge here?" he asks.

"I am," you say. "What is this about?"

"Come with me," the officer says. You walk up the road, out of earshot of the others. "Someone is letting loyalists into the city. What do you know about this?" he asks. "How are these people getting through?"

Turn the page.

Is this a trap? Does he know you're involved? It might be safer to tell the truth than to be caught lying. But if he truly doesn't know, you could get away with it.

- To tell him you know nothing about it, turn to page 89.
- To tell the truth, turn to page 91.

Though scouting might be adventurous, infantry will see more fighting. That's more your style.

Over the next few weeks, you train with the other men in a large unit. At first, the drilling and maneuvers are clumsy and disorganized. Morale is low until a new commander is brought in to lead your unit. Baron von Steuben was a Prussian general. He is a clever military leader. He quickly instills strict discipline and teaches you new maneuvers. You can see change happening before your eyes, as everyone gains skill and confidence.

One morning, some of the men at your breakfast table are talking about a rumor they've heard. "Thousands more redcoats are heading to Philadelphia," says Crosby, the man next to you.

"No doubt they're preparing for an attack," says another.

Turn the page.

Apparently, General Washington has heard the same thing. Over the next few days, the camp is abuzz with activity. Cooks are making extra food in case you need to flee. Supplies are piled near the campfires so they can be burned if the redcoats arrive. That way the British can't take them. You sense a change among the men. The confidence you felt so recently has been replaced with anxiety. Even though you've improved as soldiers, it's unknown if you can stand up to the much larger British army.

General Washington, General von Steuben, and other top officers meet in Washington's cabin regularly. Some of the men in your unit have deserted—just ran into the woods. Even some officers have left. You understand why. The alternative is waiting here to be killed. You're vulnerable here.

- To run away, turn to page 92.
- To stay and fight, turn to page 94.

You choose to be a scout. You go out on several missions, scouring the area for any sign of redcoats. When you come across colonists who are loyal to the Crown, you do whatever you can to disrupt them. You steal their food, supplies, and horses.

One mission sends you to the roads northwest of Philadelphia, an area between the city and Valley Forge. You're looking for any evidence that the redcoats may be sending scouts your way or preparing to advance.

One night, while sitting around the campfire, you hear movement in the woods. A snapped twig, a rustling bush. It seems that someone has surprised you.

Turn the page.

Your superior, Lt. Percy, points his gun into the dark. You and the other men do the same. A figure appears just outside the clearing, but you can't see them well. You hear others behind the figure. How many are there? Are they armed?

Continental soldiers around a campfire

- To shoot, turn to page 96.
- To wait for Lt. Percy to make the first move, turn to page 98.

"I haven't heard anything about this," you say. "I thought we'd been doing a very solid job of securing the area."

The officer asks you a few questions. Then he lets you go and calls Donovan over for a private talk. One by one, he interviews your men. When he's done, he walks back to you.

"Turn around," he says, taking a rope from his saddle.

"What is this?" you exclaim.

The officer ties your hands and hoists you onto the horse. "We've talked to two militias in the area, and they say the leak is here," he says. "Your men confirmed it." You look at Donovan with fury. It was all his idea, but you're going to take the fall.

Turn the page.

It's a long ride back to Valley Forge. You plead with the officers, trying to convince them of your innocence. But it's no use. Back in camp, you are whipped and then kicked out of the army. You traded a chance at a distinguished military career for a dishonorable discharge. The stain of it follows you the rest of your life.

THE END

To follow another path, turn to page 9.
To learn more about Valley Forge, turn to page 101.

These officers would not have traveled all the way out here if they didn't suspect what's going on. Your best bet is to be straight with them.

"We only did it a couple times," you say.

"Who was involved?" he asks.

"All of us," you answer.

It turns out that you are not the only ones doing this. It's a widespread problem. By being honest, you look more honorable than those at other posts who lied. Nevertheless, you can't be trusted with this duty any longer. They send you back to Valley Forge, where you are assigned to an infantry unit and trained to fight. It is not as glamorous as being in the cavalry, but at least you still get to fight for the cause you believe in.

THE END

To follow another path, turn to page 9.
To learn more about Valley Forge, turn to page 101.

You believe in the fight for independence. You are even willing to risk your life for it. But you are not willing to be a sitting duck. If the British invade here, that is what you would be.

So that night, after dark, you steal a horse, load it with supplies, and head out. You make it out of camp undetected and ride all night.

Early the next morning, you stop to rest in a thick part of the woods. After feeding your horse, you sit against a tree and eat a piece of pork and a biscuit.

You close your eyes to get some much-needed rest. The next thing you hear is the hammer of a gun cocking and a man's voice.

"Looks like we have a patriot here," the man says in a British accent.

You open your eyes. There are four or five redcoats. You look down at your Continental Army coat. You should have taken it off! The redcoats take you as a prisoner of war. You spend the rest of the war in a jail cell.

THE END

To follow another path, turn to page 9.
To learn more about Valley Forge, turn to page 101.

You'd rather die fighting for what you believe in than be a coward and run away. As it turns out, the rumors were wrong. The troop movements that Washington's spies and scouts detected were much smaller than originally thought. The redcoats are not planning to attack. That's a big relief. It gives your forces more time to train.

Troops training in Valley Forge

Over the following months, your unit improves. That June, you march to Monmouth, New Jersey, to fight the British as they move out of Philadelphia. The remaining British flee, and patriots take back the city.

For the first time since you came to Valley Forge, you feel confident about the future. America could truly become its own independent country! But that will take time. The British will not be giving up anytime soon. The war is going to last a long time. When your enlistment comes to an end, you reenlist. However long it takes, you will fight until the British are defeated.

THE END

To follow another path, turn to page 9.
To learn more about Valley Forge, turn to page 101.

You don't want to take a chance. You shoot.

You hit the person in the middle of the chest. He screams, stumbles back, and collapses. Your party rushes to the trail, guns drawn.

The man lies bleeding in the snow. He's about your age. You take away his gun, just as a woman and two kids run up. They all begin screaming and crying.

"Daddy!" the boy says, falling on top of the man.

"We need to get out of here," the lieutenant says. You are very close to Philadelphia, and all the noise may attract the wrong kind of attention. You quickly break camp and put the wounded man on a horse. You walk with the family through the night until you reach Valley Forge.

Along the way, you learn that the family are patriots. They were fleeing the redcoats in Philadelphia, looking for safety. Lt. Percy is furious with you for shooting so recklessly. The man's wife and children can't stop crying. When General Washington learns what happened, he's angry as well. You should have been cooler under pressure.

THE END

To follow another path, turn to page 9.
To learn more about Valley Forge, turn to page 101.

You point your gun at the figure and wait. Lt. Percy calls out, "Who goes there?"

"My name is Dennis Green," says the man. "I'm here with my family."

"Come forward," Percy says.

A man emerges into the light of your fire. He is dressed in clean clothing. He holds his hands out to show that he isn't holding a weapon, though he does have a pistol on his belt. "The redcoats took over my shop in Philadelphia," the man says. "But we are patriots."

The man's wife and two young children approach your group. Percy invites them to sit by the fire while they tell their story. Green ran a candle shop in town, but British soldiers took it to use as a command center. Green feared that his family would be jailed. They took what they could carry and left.

"Some redcoat scouts are camped a couple miles from here," Green says. "We passed close to them—too close." He describes the location and what kind of weapons he thinks they have.

Just before dawn, you leave the Green family behind while you seek out the redcoat camp. You catch them before they're awake and take all five members of the party prisoner. Back in Valley Forge, Lt. Percy reports your heroic efforts to General Washington. You are promoted to a higher rank. Later in the war, you're transferred back into Pulaski's cavalry. There, your talents and true patriotism truly shine.

THE END

To follow another path, turn to page 9.
To learn more about Valley Forge, turn to page 101.

CHAPTER 5

A TURNING POINT IN THE REVOLUTION

The British took control of the patriot capital of Philadelphia in the fall of 1777, two and a half years into the war. General George Washington's army had lost the capital, but they had also surprised the British with how well they fought. The winter in Valley Forge could either make or break the ragtag Continental Army. Many among the more than 12,000 people who settled there in December felt hopeful about the future.

The Continental Army was made up of men from all walks of life. Folks from the country and the city, from the north and the south. They were laborers, tradesmen, fishers, and farmers. There were those who were wealthy and those of more modest means. Native people, immigrants, and free and formerly enslaved Black people served in the army.

The camp also hosted about 400 women and children who had followed the army to be with their loved ones. At first, General Washington did not want these families with the army. He thought they would slow down troop movements.

Washington later realized how valuable they could be. Women helped with nursing, cooking, and laundry. They mended clothing, sold provisions, served as housekeepers, and more. Some women even helped in battle loading artillery.

One of the first things that Washington ordered when the army arrived at Valley Forge was the construction of log cabins. They built about 2,000 small wooden shelters. The cabins were aligned into rows, with a sort of road between each row. The men also built forts, a bridge over the Schuylkill River, and trenches for going to the bathroom.

In the early weeks, food was shipped to the camps. For the most part, they had enough to eat. But there were periods of shortages. The worst was in February. When supplies ran low, many went hungry. As for clothing, some of the men had enough, but others did not. At one point in March, nearly 3,000 men were listed as unfit for duty due to lack of sufficient clothing. No battles were fought at Valley Forge, but about 2,000 people died from diseases such as smallpox, influenza, and typhoid fever.

General Washington was an inspiring figure to many in camp, but he was not the only one. He persuaded a former Prussian officer, Baron Friedrich Wilhelm von Steuben, to come to the camp and train the troops. Von Steuben taught the troops new skills and how to fight as a unit. His reforms became the foundation for the modern U.S. Army.

Another important international figure in camp was Casimir Pulaski, a Polish military commander. Pulaski had fought in Poland for that country's independence and had come to the United States to help in its cause.

Pulaski was a highly skilled horseman. During the winter in Valley Forge, he reformed the Continental Army's cavalry, writing its first regulations. He has been called the father of the American cavalry.

The patriots stayed in Valley Forge from December 1777 until June 1778. Upon learning that the British were leaving Philadelphia, they marched out on June 19 to pursue them. The patriots defeated the British at the Battle of Monmouth, New Jersey, on June 28.

Though the war would last another five years, it was a significant moment. By successfully guiding his troops through the winter at Valley Forge and significantly improving the military, Washington had proved his worth as the commander in chief. The capital was back under patriot control. The patriots had perhaps never felt more confident.

Timeline of the American Revolution

April 19, 1775: The first shots of the Revolutionary War are fired in Massachusetts.

July 4, 1776: America declares its independence.

Fall 1776: The British win a series of battles, pushing Washington's troops out of New York and New Jersey.

September 26, 1777: The British take Philadelphia.

October 4, 1777: Washington's troops lose the Battle of Germantown.

December 1777: Washington and his army arrive at Valley Forge.

February 1778: France enters the war on the side of the Americans.

February 23, 1778: Baron non Steuben arrives at Valley Forge to take charge of military training.

June 18, 1778: The British abandon Philadelphia.

June 28, 1778: The Continental Army defeats the British in the Battle of Monmouth.

September–October 1781: French and American troops defeat a large British army at the Battle of Yorktown.

September 3, 1783: The Treaty of Paris officially ends the War for Independence.

Other Paths to Explore

1. One of the challenges at Valley Forge was for the diverse types of people to find a way to get along. With people from so many different walks of life, they saw the world differently and disagreed on many things. Imagine you were General George Washington. What ideas might you have had to unite the soldiers?

2. Imagine what life was like for the patriots in Philadelphia after the British took the city. What would you have done in that situation? Would you have pretended to be loyal to the British? Would you have fled the city? Or would you have tried to serve as a spy for the Continental Army and help them in any way you can? Why?

3. There were many children living with their families at Valley Forge. Imagine what it would be like to be a child in a military encampment. How might you help out? What might you do for fun?

Bibliography

American Battlefield Trust: Winter at Valley Forge
battlefields.org/learn/articles/winter-valley-forge

American Battlefield Trust: Women at Valley Forge
battlefields.org/learn/articles/women-valley-forge

Drury, Bob, and Tom Clavin. *Valley Forge*. New York: Simon & Schuster, 2018.

Loane, Nancy K. *Following the Drum: Women at the Valley Forge Encampment*. Washington, DC: Potomac Books, Inc., 2009.

National Park Service: Valley Forge/American Indian Allies at Valley Forge
nps.gov/vafo/learn/historyculture/americanindians.htm

National Park Service: Valley Forge/Patriots of Color at Valley Forge
nps.gov/vafo/learn/historyculture/patriotsofcoloratvalleyforge.htm

National Park Service: Valley Forge/The Women Present at Valley Forge
nps.gov/vafo/learn/historyculture/valleyforgewomen.htm

Trickey, Erick. "The Prussian Nobleman Who Helped Save the American Revolution." *Smithsonian Magazine*, April 26, 2017.
smithsonianmag.com/history/baron-von-steuben-180963048/

Glossary

cavalry (KA-vuhl-ree)—soldiers who fight on horseback

desert (di-ZUHRT)—to leave military service without permission

detachment (dee-TACH-muhnt)—a group of soldiers chosen from a larger group for a special purpose

dysentery (DI-sen-tayr-ee)—a serious infection of the intestines that can be deadly

infirmary (in-FURM-uh-ree)—a place where sick or injured people receive care

influenza (in-floo-EN-zuh)—an illness that is like a bad cold with fever and muscle pain; a virus causes influenza

loyalist (LOI-uh-list)—a colonist who was loyal to Great Britain during the Revolutionary War

maneuver (muh-NOO-ver)—a strategic military movement

Prussian (PRUH-shuhn)—from Prussia, which is now part of Germany

smallpox (SMAWL-poks)—contagious disease that causes people's skin to break out in blisters and leaves deep scars

typhoid fever (TYE-foid FEE-vur)—a serious infectious disease that sometimes leads to death

variolation (vay-ree-uh-LAY-shuhn)—infecting someone with a small amount of a virus in order to vaccinate them against it

Read More

Braun, Eric. *The Real George Washington: the Truth Behind the Legend.* North Mankato, MN: Compass Point Books, 2019.

Freedman, Russell. *Washington at Valley Forge.* New York: Holiday House, 2020.

Waldvogel, K.M. *Spies, Soldiers, Couriers, & Saboteurs: Women of the American Revolution.* Waukesha, WI: Orange Hat Publishing, 2019.

Internet Sites

Ducksters: American Revolution/Valley Forge
ducksters.com/history/american_revolution/valley_forge.php

History.com: Valley Forge
history.com/topics/american-revolution/valley-forge

National Park Service: Valley Forge for Kids
nps.gov/vafo/learn/kidsyouth/index.htm

JOIN OTHER HISTORICAL ADVENTURES WITH MORE
YOU CHOOSE SEEKING HISTORY!

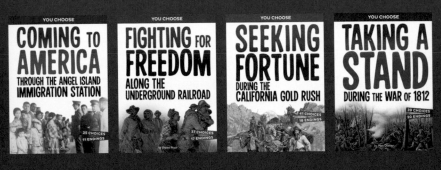

About the Author

Eric Braun is a children's author and editor. He has written dozens of books on many topics, and one of his books was read by an astronaut on the International Space Station for kids on Earth to watch. Eric lives in Minneapolis with his wife, two kids, and a dog who is afraid of cardboard.